POSITION AND FINGERING CHART

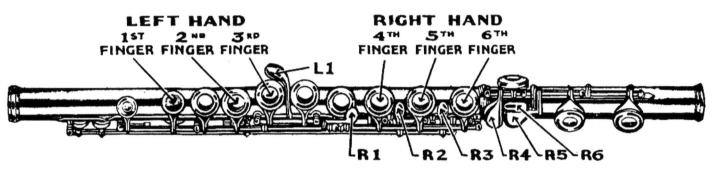

Study the pictures above for correct position of lips and fingers. Also learn to use the fingering chart on this page. A black dot indicates the corresponding key is to be closed, and a circle that it is to be open. The letters "R" or "L" in connection with a number show what additional key or keys should be used, and whether the key is operated by a right or left hand finger. The letter "T" means the thumb should be placed on the right of the two thumb keys.

When you have finished this book, you should secure a complete flute chart, which will show additional fingerings.

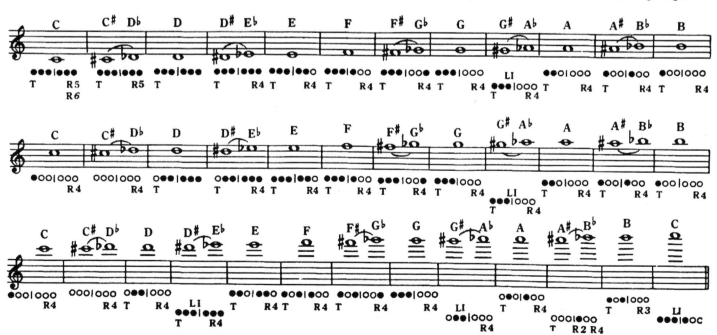

70203

LESSON 1

① **WHOLE NOTES AND RESTS**

Whole note
4 counts. Whole rest
4 counts. Notice the whole rest hangs under the line.

②

Watch each note or rest as you count it.

③

Be sure you tongue each note.

④ **HALF NOTES**

Half notes—2 counts each.

⑤

⑥ **HALF RESTS**

Half rest—2 counts. Notice the half rest lies above the line.

⑦

⑧ **QUARTER NOTES**

Quarter notes—1 count each.

⑨

Count each note—don't guess.

A HIGHER TONE

What is the name of the new tone?

Count slowly and steadily.

Breath should be taken through the corners of the mouth.

Correct position of body and instrument is important.

Do you tongue each note?

THE ROCKING CHAIR

HAPPY LANDINGS

Try naming these notes.

A NUT TO CRACK

Look at the rests carefully.

Easy Steps to the Band—*C Flute*

LESSON 3

A LOWER TONE

②

Are you sitting and holding your instrument correctly?

③

Can you name these notes?

④

Count carefully.

QUARTER RESTS

Quarter rest—1 count.

TIME OUT

THE MERRY - GO - ROUND

DOTS

Dotted half note—3 counts

Easy Steps to the Band—*C Flute*

GOING HIGHER

SCHOOL BELLS

What kind of notes are these? 3/4 time has three beats in each measure.

THE SWAN

Try naming the notes.

LULLABY

STEPS

COASTING

SKIPS

WATCH YOUR STEP

Count each note and rest carefully.

Easy Steps to the Band—*C Flute*

LESSON 5

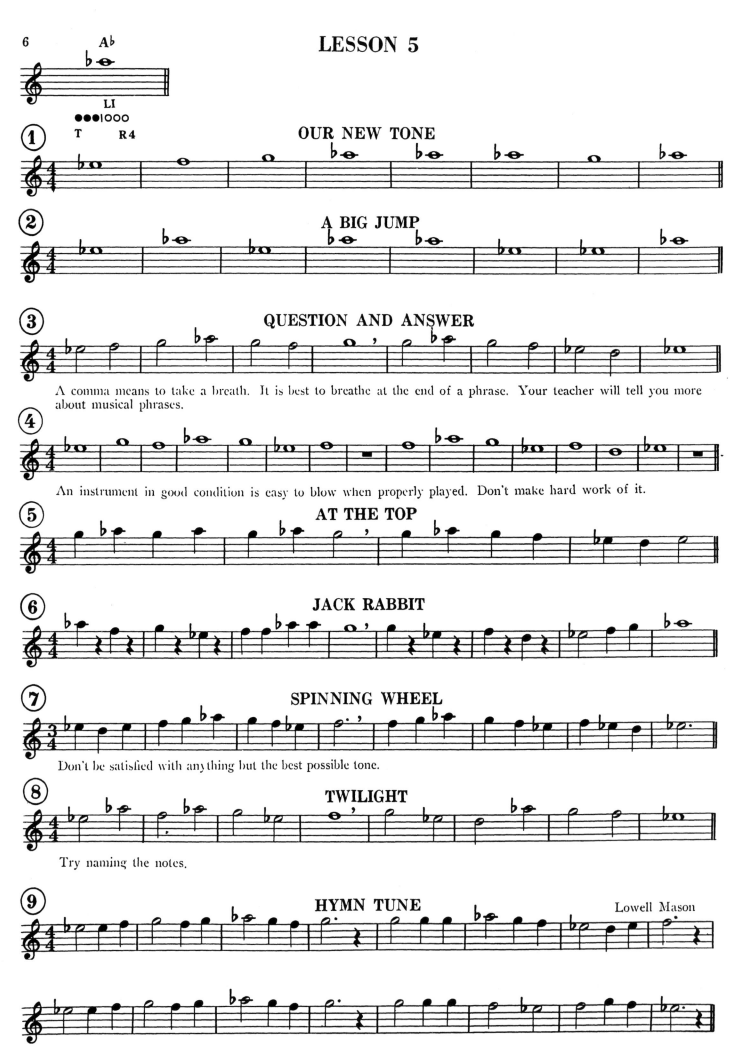

OUR NEW TONE

A BIG JUMP

QUESTION AND ANSWER

A comma means to take a breath. It is best to breathe at the end of a phrase. Your teacher will tell you more about musical phrases.

An instrument in good condition is easy to blow when properly played. Don't make hard work of it.

AT THE TOP

JACK RABBIT

SPINNING WHEEL

Don't be satisfied with anything but the best possible tone.

TWILIGHT

Try naming the notes.

HYMN TUNE

Lowell Mason

Easy Steps to the Band—*C Flute*

LESSON 6

A NEW TONE

1. What are the names of these tones?

HIGH JUMP

2.

ANOTHER NEW TONE

3. Name the new tones.

THE DIVER

4. Are you breathing through the corners of your mouth?

5.

THE CHURN

6. Are your fingers in good position?

HERE AND THERE

7. Name these notes.

TEAMWORK

8.

ON THE MARCH

9. Be sure you are right, then work for speed.

MARY HAD A LITTLE LAMB

10.

The flute part to No. 10 can be played with all instruments except B♭ saxophones, oboes, and horns.

LESSON 7

Sometimes 4/4 time is indicated by the sign C.

JOYOUS DAYS

EVENING

In measures 3 and 4 some instruments have a different part.

CLIMBING

Two dots before a double bar means to repeat.

SWINGING

A curved line connecting two notes of the same pitch is called a tie and makes the two notes sound as one.

OLD McDONALD

The flute part to Nos. 8 and 9 can be played with all instruments except oboes, Bb saxophones, horns, and basses.

OLD RUSSIAN SONG

REVIEW OF ALL NOTES LEARNED
(For individual use only)

Easy Steps to the Band—*C Flute*

Keep trying to improve your tone.

OVER THE MOUNTAINS

Some instruments have other notes in the last three measures.

Is your position good? Refer to the photograph on the first page.

This is good practice—try it often.

JUMPING JACK

Often two equal tones must be played in one beat. Practice repeating two short tones to a beat until you can play them evenly. Let some of the class play one tone to a beat while the others play two tones to a beat. Finger the note in No. 7 so all can practice together.

YANKEE DOODLE

Early American Song

FIDDLE - DEE - DEE

J. W. Elliot

In this method no attempt has been made to put commas at every place a breath should or may be taken. Commas simply indicate that a breath taken at that point will help with the phrasing.

Eighth notes—2 equal tones in one count.

Tongue the notes lightly.

2/4 time has two counts in each measure.

BUSY BEES

Are you counting the time correctly?

UNISON

When all instruments play the same part, we say they are in unison.

LIGHTLY ROW   Folk Tune

HARMONY

Different parts sounding well together make what is called harmony.

WINTER SONG

A flat (♭) lowers a tone ½ step. A sharp (♯) raises a tone ½ step. A natural (♮) means the tone is not to be sharped or flatted.

Sharps or flats placed at the beginning of a piece should be used all through the piece. They are known as the "key signature." In the future always look for it before you begin to play.

Did you look at the signature?

Name the notes.

Measure repeat sign—play the measure before over again.

Nos. 6 and 7 may be used together as a duet.

PLEYEL'S HYMN
(harmonized)

Ignace Pleyel

POLLY WOLLY DOODLE
(Adapted)

College Song

Easy Steps to the Band—*C Flute*

12

LESSON 11

The letters D C. stand for the Italian words *Da Capo*, which mean "go back to the beginning." *Al* means "to." *Fine* is Italian for "Finish." Therefore, D.C. al Fine means "go back to the beginning and play to *Fine*." ⌒ placed over a double bar means the same as *Fine*.

Look at the signature. Can you name the notes?

Easy Steps to the Band—*C Flute*

THERE'S MUSIC IN THE AIR
(harmonized)

George F. Root

The first measure is not complete. Notes of incomplete measures at the beginning of a piece are often called "pick-up" notes or "start" notes.

Notice the difference in signature between No. 7 and No. 8. First be sure you are playing correctly, then work for speed.

LONG, LONG AGO

T. H. Bailey

LESSON 13

A LONG JOURNEY

Is your position good?

SLUMBER SONG

Eighth notes may be written separately this way. ♪

Count 2 for the dotted quarter note—the eighth note comes after the 2nd beat.

FOLK SONG

ABIDE WITH ME

W. H. Monk

MINUET

MARCHING TUNE

CHROMATIC MELODY

SCALE MELODY

Count carefully.

AMERICA

Henry Carey

3/4 ACCOMPANIMENT

An accompaniment is a part or parts used to form a musical background for a melody.

ROUND—ARE YOU SLEEPING

No. 9 may be played all together or as a round.

LESSON 15

VESPER HYMN

T. Moore

THE SUNSHINE SONG

Count carefully.

GERMAN WALTZ
(melody)

German Folk Song

The letter *p* stands for the Italian word *piano*, which means "soft."

The letter *f* stands for the Italian word *forte*, which means "loud."

GERMAN WALTZ
(harmony)

German Folk Song

This part may be used with the melody above.

THE DUSTMAN

Johannes Brahms

Look out for the new signature.

Nos. 2, 3, 4, 5, 6, and 7 may be played together.

An eighth note followed by an eighth rest. Play a short tone on the beat.

The eighth rests take the place of the eighth notes in No. 6.

1ST AND 2ND ENDINGS

Play through the 1st ending and repeat. The second time, skip the 1st ending and play the 2nd ending

GERMAN FOLK SONG

AULD LANG SYNE

Scotch Folk Song

Fine

D.S. stands for the Italian words *Dal Segno* and means to go back to this sign %

D. S. al Fine

STEAL AWAY
(adapted)
(4-part harmony)

Negro Melody

"A" part

Fine

D. S. al Fine

LESSON 17

A curved line connecting notes of different pitch is called a "slur." Tongue the first note and continue blowing while you finger the remaining notes of the slur.

Watch out for signature changes.

Be sure you are right, then work for speed on Nos. 6, 7, 8, and 9.

GLIDING ALONG

Notice the slurs.

THE TICKING CLOCK

Moderato

Moderato means to play at a moderate speed.

INTEGER VITAE
(The Upright Man)

F. F. Flemming

Watch for slurs.

BLOW THE MAN DOWN

Sailors' Song

Easy Steps to the Band—*C Flute*

MELODY

Allegro means "quick or lively."

2/4 ACCOMPANIMENT

2/4 ACCOMPANIMENT

Nos. 5, 6, and 7 should be learned separately, then used together if there are three or more in the class.

STARS OF THE SUMMER NIGHT

Isaac D. Woodbury

Crescendo, indicated by *cres.* or ⟨, means to get gradually louder.
Diminuendo, indicated by *dim.* or ⟩, means to get gradually softer.

OLD DOG TRAY

Stephen Foster

On the beat.

Eighth rests followed by eighth notes are often called "after-beats." Notice the rest comes on the beat.

Nos. 1, 2, and 3 may be played together.

Be sure you are right, then work for speed.

Nos. 1, 2, and 3 may be played together for comparison.

HAPPY JOE

Your teacher will explain how the pick-up notes should be played.

Are you slurring correctly?

ALMA MATER   College Song

mf is for *mezzo forte*, which means "medium volume." *ff* is for *fortissimo*, which means "very loud."

From "The Heavens are Telling" — Haydn

Accent (*Fortzando—fz* or *sfz*)—tongue sharply, then gradually soften the tone.

From "Amaryllis" — Ghys

Staccato—tongue the tone lightly and make it shorter than written. A dash means to hold the note full value.

From "Chanson Triste" — Tschaikowsky

Legato—tongue softly, using the syllable "dōō." There should be no pause between tones.

Easy Steps to the Band—*C Flute*

1 Half Note tied to an eighth note—learn it well because it is used often.

5 / **6** Dotted eighths followed by sixteenths—one beat for two notes with the first sounding much longer than the second. The difference between Nos. 5 and 6 should be clearly heard.

11 Andante — GAUDEAMUS — Old College Song

The word *Andante* indicates the piece is to be played a little slower than *Moderato*.

12 LITTLE BROWN CHURCH IN THE VALE
(2-part harmony)

Easy Steps to the Band—*C Flute*

LESSON 21

No. 4 is part of the chromatic scale. A chromatic scale moves by half steps.

Sixteenth notes—play 4 equal tones to a count.

Nos. 7 and 8 must *not* sound alike.

MARYLAND, MY MARYLAND

LISTEN TO THE MOCKING BIRD

A. Hawthorne

6/8 time may be counted in 2 ways. In slow music, ♪ usually gets 1 beat; in fast music, ♩. gets 1 beat. Practice this both ways. Your teacher will tell you more about 6/8 time.

ROUND—ROW, ROW, ROW YOUR BOAT

FOR HE'S A JOLLY GOOD FELLOW

Fine

D. C. al Fine

POP GOES THE WEASEL

Alla Breve—commonly called "cut time". ♩ gets one beat.

Compare with No. 3.

Compare with No. 5.

Compare with No. 7.

Compare with No. 9.

Compare with No. 11.

Compare with No. 13.

OUT THE WINDOW HE MUST GO

THE GIRL I LEFT BEHIND ME

Irish Jig

LESSON 25

When the accent falls in unusual places, we say the music is syncopated.

Nos. 1, 2, and 3 may be played together.

Syncopation.

No. 5 may be played with No. 4 for comparison.

No. 6 may be played with No. 5 for comparison.

CARRY ME BACK TO OLD VIRGINNY

J. A. Bland

This, (♪·♫) turned around becomes ♫·♪. Still one beat, but the short tone comes on the beat.

COMIN' THRO' THE RYE

Scotch Melody

Triplet - 3 equal tones in one beat.   No. 11 will require very careful practice.

JUANITA

Spanish Air

MARCH FROM AIDA

Verdi

Easy Steps to the Band—*C Flute*

CHROMATIC SCALE

SPECIAL SOLOS AND DUETS

CRADLE SONG

Brahms

COUNTRY GARDENS

English Folk Dance

EASY HARMONIZED PIECES

EASY STEPS MARCH

CHORAL

Henry K. Oliver 1832

AMERICA

Henry Carey

OUR BOYS WILL SHINE

AMERICA, THE BEAUTIFUL

Samuel A. Ward

Easy Steps to the Band—*C Flute*

SHADOWLAND
Waltz

Fine

D. C. al Fine

THE JUNIOR BAND
March

OUR SCHOOL
March

SUNSET MEDITATIONS
Tone Poem

CARNIVAL KING
Overture

THE SALUTE
March